COLLEGE READINESS 101

COLLEGE READINESS 101

A College & Career Workbook
For The High School Sophomore

EDITOR

Dr. Serena C. Walker

GRAPHIC DESIGNER

Purposely Created Publishing Group

ILLUSTRATOR

Phillip Sidberry

ISBN-13: 978-0-692-13733-8

Printed in the United States of America

10 9 8 7 6 5 4 3 2 1

First Edition

www.collegereadiness101.com

Acknowledgements

This workbook is dedicated to the people in my life that have poured their support into me and my passion for assisting students with pursuing their educational goals.

TABLE OF CONTENTS

INTRODUCTION

The college admissions process can seem overwhelming. However, it doesn't have to be intimidating if you have a strategic plan. This college readiness workbook will allow you to design a strategy for college acceptance specific to what you want your college experience to be.

I will challenge you to take a good look at yourself and where you stand in reference to the requirements for your top college choices. This workbook is designed to equip you to become a successful college student by exposing you to major concepts in college readiness and career planning.

This workbook is intended to assist high school sophomores, and their parents, in navigating the college admissions and acceptance processes. By completing this workbook, you will have a better understanding of what you should do to better prepare yourself for a college education. This workbook has 3 sections:

The College Readiness Program and Activities

The College Readiness Program and Activities section of the workbook is designed to introduce you to concepts you might not be familiar with, or reiterate concepts you have already learned through conversations with your family or high school counselor. In this section, you will find college readiness program content, as well as tips, suggestions, research activities, and areas for notes.

The Sophomore Resources & Tools

The Sophomore Resources & Tools section has creative documents that you can use throughout your college readiness process to assist you along the way. In this section, you will find a student brag sheet, checklists, testing tips, and more.

The College & Career Plan

The College & Career Plan is where you will document activities that you have completed towards your college preparatory plan. You will find a monthly calendar and space to input your tasks in a journal entry format. Upon completion of the College & Career Plan section, you will have a self-designed guide to follow throughout the rest of your high school career.

CHAPTER 1

YOUR SOPHOMORE YEAR

One down, three to go!

This is generally a good year for most students. Sophomores can usually lie below the radar. You are currently in between the two attention-driven years in high school. The new freshmen are now getting your previous newbie attention and the juniors are now starting to receive the major college prep information.

Take this year to focus on boosting your GPA and increasing your extracurricular activities. This is a great year to begin thinking about alterative class options as well. We'll discuss those a little later in the workbook.

Are there any concerns or questions that you have in reference to what to expect this year? Record them here.

1. _____

2. _____

3. _____

4. _____

5. _____

Getting To Know The Sophomore Student

To assess you as a student, I will need to know a little bit about you. By profiling yourself, you will gather information that will assist you with understanding where you are currently in relation to where you want to be. Knowing your demographic information, academic profile, future plans, and current strengths and weaknesses will be vital to making informed decisions and determining potential opportunities. Did any of your plans change since your freshman year?

While many students may have somewhat of a guide to follow in the college selection process due to having parents that went to college, others may be on track to be **first generation** college students. These are students who will be the first in their immediate family to attend college. If this is you, it's good to know that most colleges are investing in the success of first generation college students and will provide a number of extra resources to assist you through your college career.

Also, during your sophomore year, some colleges will allow you to start taking **dual enrollment** courses. These are courses that you can take to receive high school and college credit at the same time. Many students are starting to take advantage of this opportunity while they are in high school. The great thing about dual enrollment courses is that once you get to college, you are already ahead of your classmates.

Take a few minutes to complete the Sophomore Student Profile. You may want to review it with your high school counselor, graduation coach, or a trusted adult to start understanding what you, as a student, look like on paper.

Sophomore Student Profile

First Name: _____ MI. _____ Last Name: _____

High School: _____ Gender: _____

Age: _____

Ethnicity:

❑ Hispanic or Latino
❑ Non-Hispanic or Latino

Race:

❑ American Indian or Alsaskan
❑ Asian
❑ African American/Black
❑ Native Hawaiian or Pacific Islander
❑ White

9th Grade Performance

❑ Final English/Language Arts Grade: _____

❑ Final Math Grade: _____

❑ Final Science Grade: _____

❑ Final Social Studies Grade: _____

❑ Other Class: _____: _____

❑ Other Class: _____: _____

❑ Other Class: _____: _____

Are you taking any Honors or AP Courses this year?

❑ Yes

❑ No

Are you taking any Dual Enrollment Courses this year?

❑ Yes

❑ No

I will be a 1st Generation College Student: ❑ Yes ❑ No

Strength Classes:

1. _____

2. _____

3. _____

Career Aspirations:

1. _____

2. _____

3. _____

Weakness Classes:

1. _____

2. _____

3. _____

Who will assist you with this college prep process?

1. _____

2. _____

3. _____

While this is just a simple profile of you and your performance from ninth grade, now that you see yourself on paper, how would you assess yourself if you were a teacher, counselor, or college recruiter?

Self-Evaluation	**Why did you give yourself this score?**
❏ 10	_____
❏ 9	_____
❏ 8	_____
❏ 7	_____
❏ 6	_____
❏ 5	
❏ 4	
❏ 3	
❏ 2	
❏ 1	

Again, now that you see yourself on paper, what are some things that you think you can continue to build upon for the rest of your high school career?

1. _____

2. _____

3. _____

4. _____

5. _____

College Readiness by Grade

As you can understand, students in different grades will need to focus on different parts of their college readiness process. Now that you have completed your freshman year in high school, it's time that we refine the tasks that you will need to complete this year.

This list is a general overview of what students should do throughout their sophomore year in high school. It is imperative that you and your parents create goals for each **academic year**. Assess your performance and evaluate the goals met or unmet at the end of this year. Use the upcoming summer to finalize activities and set the goals for your junior year.

The best advice that educational professionals have for students thinking about going to college is to START EARLY! As a sophomore, you may think you have time to get things together later. However, as I say to all students, while you are waiting around, your peers from all over the country are positioning themselves to take advantage of their college preparatory opportunities. It is never too early to prepare for a college education.

When it comes to understanding the high school years and setting your goals, think of your matriculation as a track athlete running a 400-meter race. There are strategies that an athlete practices daily to leverage the best opportunity for success. You will need to do the same to **matriculate** successfully through high school and prepare for college.

400 METER RACE

Runners will start in the blocks, staggered from the runner in front of them and the one behind. Once the gun goes off, runners will use the first 100 meters as an opportunity to set a pace for the entire race.

STUDENT MATRICULATION

Just like your freshman year, all students will not be on the same level academically, socially, or financially, but everyone is running the same race. This is your year to set your pace of your entire high school career.

400 METER RACE

The second 100 meters is the back straight away that allows runners to see how far ahead or behind they are from the other runners. Basically they can evaluate where they are and make adjustments if needed.

STUDENT MATRICULATION

As a sophomore, you already have gone through the obstacles of being new to the school and can now operate with more confidence. This year, most students coast to get an overview of how the rest of their high school years will go.

400 METER RACE

The third 100 meters is the hardest part of the race because that's when the "bear" jumps on your back. Your legs get heavy and it becomes hard to keep your pace. It's a curve, so the runner has to lean into it to get the best opportunity of coming out with an advantage.

STUDENT MATRICULATION

With a lot of pressure and focus on the junior year, students may begin to feel stressed about juggling more difficult academic courses, standardized testing, social life, and college readiness. Students will need to lean in and give extra effort through this tough year to be successful.

400 METER RACE

During the last 100 meters, you can see the finish line but it is still a ways away. Since your energy is now drained, it takes the training you have had throughout your daily practices to stay focused, keep your form, push through, and cross the finish line.

STUDENT MATRICULATION

Just like the last 100 meters in a race, seniors may find themselves slowing down, getting distracted by the crowd, and giving up right before the finish line. Don't let senioritis cost you the race. Students will need to stay focused, commit to their goal, and use the hard work and lessons learned to get them to graduation.

COLLEGE READINESS ACTIVITIES FOR SOPHOMORES

Now that you have a year under your belt, you should be better equipped to maneuver through routine high school matters. Many high school students describe the tenth grade as a coasting year. There aren't a lot of hard classes and heavy pressure during this year. However, if this is not your experience, you will need to buckle down and do the things necessary for you to be successful.

Hopefully, your established work ethic and study skills are strong enough to carry you through your high school years. If not, review the study skills tips in the Student Resource & Tools section of the workbook. You are not expected to know the exact college you want to attend, your specific program of study, or what career you want to pursue at this time. However, you should be thinking about it. Here is a list of tasks that you should complete this year:

LOOKING AT POTENTIAL COLLEGE OPTIONS

This year will be the year that your family and teachers will consistently talk to you about college. Start looking at potential college options and have a list of schools you might want to visit in the future. If you have older siblings that are already in college or soon will be, ask them about their experiences and what they wish they would have done, or not done, to prepare for college.

What are some of your top colleges so far?

1. _____

2. _____

3. _____

4. _____

5. _____

CONTINUE BEING ACTIVE WITH EXTRACURRICULAR ACTIVITIES

It is important that you are an active student outside of the classroom. Colleges are looking for well-rounded individuals to become the face of their institution. With that being said, find out what activities will be best for you: joining a sports team, band, club, or organization; starting a part-time job; volunteering your time and talents at the local Boys and Girls Club, church, or food pantry, etc. Your extracurricular activities could be something that gets you accepted into a college, or qualifies you as a finalist for a scholarship. As a sophomore, you may not be able to play a leadership role in some of the organizations. However, find out how to get on the leadership track.

What extracurricular activities will you participate in this year?

1. _____

2. _____

3. _____

4. _____

5. _____

START GATHERING INFORMATION ABOUT FINANCING A COLLEGE EDUCATION

Begin to research with your parents and/or high school counselor about how you can pay for your college education. Hopefully, you will do well academically or athletically, and will be eligible for an array of scholarships. Everyone wants scholarships! However, the reality is that not everyone will get one. With that being said, it's important to explore and identify alternative ways to pay for your education. Student grants, loans and part-time jobs may be viable options.

What options will you explore in reference to paying for your college education?

1. _____

2. _____

3. _____

4. _____

5. _____

6. _____

7. _____

8. _____

9. _____

10. _____

EXPLORE OTHER ACADEMIC OPTIONS

Students who are doing well may want to explore taking more rigorous classes, including **advanced placement** courses or honors courses. These courses look great on a college application. Also, you may want to start researching **dual enrollment** programs. As stated before, dual enrollment courses allow students to get college credit and high school credit for the same course. Research these options to see if they fit in your college preparatory plan. Also, talk to your counselor to see if this a good option for your current academic rigor.

Do you plan to take any AP, Honors, or Dual Enrollment courses this year? ☐ Yes   ☐ No

If so, which classes do you plan to take?

1. _____

2. _____

3. _____

4. _____

5. _____

6. _____

7. _____

TALK TO YOUR PARENTS OR GUARDIANS ABOUT YOUR GOALS

In my experience, generally parents start the conversation about the future. They are the ones doing the research and encouraging the student to want better for themselves. However, everyone's household is different. Some students will have lots of support at home, while others will have to do a lot on their own. Some families will have the means to pay for a college education out-of-pocket, others will have to take out loans and/or get part-time jobs. Whatever your household situation may be, you have to start planning and setting your goals. Take some time to begin researching a few things about going to college and discuss it with your parent(s), guardian(s), or trusted adult. Showing initiative about your future will be a great step forward.

What are some topics you can discuss with your parents about going to college?

1. _____

2. _____

3. _____

4. _____

5. _____

6. _____

7. _____

8. _____

9. _____

10. _____

ASSESS YOUR CAREER ASPIRATIONS

One of the major goals of attaining a college degree is to place yourself in a better position for employment and financial stability in the future. You wouldn't want to do all of the research papers, lab classes, and internships just to get a job that you could have gotten right out of high school, right? Take the time to explore some career opportunities you may be interested in. Make a list of potential positions and begin to research the ins and outs of them.

What are some careers that you are interested in, and why?

1. _____

Why: _____

_____

2. _____

Why: _____

_____

3. _____

Why: _____

_____

4. _____

Why: _____

_____

Goal Setting Is Critical

Now that you are matriculating through high school, you are going to have a lot of conversations about your future. You probably have already begun those conversations. As stated in the freshman workbook… without goals or a destination, you are just sailing in the wind. You will need to establish some direction for where you want to go.

First, we must begin with the fact that these goals should be your own. Your parents, teachers, and friends will play a role in refining your goals. However, when it's all said and done, your goals are for you and you alone. You will need to set goals based on what is important to you. It's essential that they are important to you because you will have to articulate why you have set these goals for yourself. Sometimes, you may have to defend your position on your goals.

Secondly, we need to make sure you are setting S.M.A.R.T. Goals. This means that they are:

1. **Specific**: Clear and well defined goals are paramount to success. Unclear or vague goals allow you too much wiggle room and usually end up in failure.

2. **Measurable**: You will need to connect a number or an amount to your goals. This will allow you to measure your progress as you continue through your high school years.

3. **Attainable**: You have to set goals that you can attain - goals that you know you can reach. Setting unattainable goals will kill your morale and eagerness to continue.

4. **Relevant**: Your goals should be relevant to where you want to go. This will keep you focused and diligently working towards it.

5. **Time-Bound**: You must give yourself a deadline to reach your goals. Prioritizing will keep you accountable. This will be very important when you start to have multiple goals competing for your time.

Lastly, the most effective task you can do when it comes to setting goals is to write them down. This makes them real. You must be willing to keep yourself accountable for doing what you said you were going to do. Now, you can visit them periodically to assess your progress.

Take a few minutes to write down some S.M.A.R.T. sophomore year goals.

Sophomore Year Goals

S.M.A.R.T. Academic Goals

1. _____

2. _____

3. _____

4. _____

5. _____

S.M.A.R.T. Extracurricular Goals

1. _____

2. _____

3. _____

4. _____

5. _____

S.M.A.R.T. Miscellaneous Goals

1. _____

2. _____

3. _____

4. _____

5. _____

Sophomore Year Course Selection

It is very important to have a strong academic year as a sophomore. As many students have said, it's their easiest year. Take advantage of the opportunities this year will bring. You will need to continue to build a cushion for the ever-important junior year. Let's start with your class selection. Consider the following questions:

1. What classes do you plan to take?

2. What classes will your high school offer during your sophomore year?

3. Do you know what classes you should take based on your graduation goals?

4. Do you plan to take any honors or dual enrollment courses?

5. Which classes can you be most successful in?

Use the Selected Sophomore Year Classes Form to document the course you selected for your sophomore year. Remember to come back to this form to write your final grades beside them. You will also see two other forms to project your classes for your junior and senior courses within the Sophomore Resources & Tools section of the workbook.

Selected Sophomore Year Classes

English/Language Arts:

- ❑ American Literature
- ❑ British Literature
- ❑ Comparative Literature
- ❑ Composition
- ❑ Contemporary Literature
- ❑ Creative Writing
- ❑ Debate
- ❑ Journalism
- ❑ Poetry
- ❑ Rhetoric
- ❑ World Literature
- ❑ _____
- ❑ _____

Foreign Language:

- ❑ American Sign Language
- ❑ Arabic
- ❑ Chinese
- ❑ French
- ❑ German
- ❑ Italian
- ❑ Japanese
- ❑ Korean
- ❑ Latin
- ❑ Portuguese
- ❑ Russian
- ❑ Spanish
- ❑ _____
- ❑ _____

Honors or AP Courses:

- ❑ _____
- ❑ _____
- ❑ _____
- ❑ _____
- ❑ _____

Mathematics:

- ❑ Algebra 1
- ❑ Algebra 2
- ❑ Calculus
- ❑ Geometry
- ❑ Integrated Math
- ❑ Pre-Algebra
- ❑ Pre-Calculus
- ❑ Statistics
- ❑ Trigonometry
- ❑ _____
- ❑ _____

CTAE:

- ❑ Accounting
- ❑ Auto Repair
- ❑ Business
- ❑ Computer Science
- ❑ Cosmetology
- ❑ Culinary Arts
- ❑ Entrepreneurship
- ❑ Fashion Design
- ❑ Graphic Design
- ❑ Healthcare
- ❑ JROTC
- ❑ Law/Criminal Justice
- ❑ Marketing
- ❑ Music Production
- ❑ Nutrition
- ❑ Robotics
- ❑ Web Design
- ❑ Welding
- ❑ Wood Working
- ❑ _____
- ❑ _____

Science:

- ❑ Anatomy & Physiology
- ❑ Astronomy
- ❑ Biology
- ❑ Botany
- ❑ Chemistry
- ❑ Earth Science
- ❑ Environmental Science
- ❑ Forensic Science
- ❑ Life Science
- ❑ Oceanography
- ❑ Organic Chemistry
- ❑ Physical Science
- ❑ Physics
- ❑ Zoology
- ❑ _____
- ❑ _____

Physical Education:

- ❑ Aerobics
- ❑ Gymnastics
- ❑ Health
- ❑ Physical Education
- ❑ Swimming
- ❑ Wellness
- ❑ Weight Training
- ❑ _____
- ❑ _____

Visual Arts:

- ❑ Art
- ❑ Art History
- ❑ Digital Media
- ❑ Drawing
- ❑ Film Production/Video
- ❑ Photography
- ❑ _____
- ❑ _____

Social Studies:

- ❑ American History
- ❑ Anthropology
- ❑ Current Events
- ❑ Economics
- ❑ European History
- ❑ Geography
- ❑ International Relations
- ❑ Political Science
- ❑ Psychology
- ❑ Religious Studies
- ❑ Sociology
- ❑ US Government
- ❑ World History
- ❑ World Religions
- ❑ _____
- ❑ _____

Performing Arts:

- ❑ Choir
- ❑ Concert Band
- ❑ Dance
- ❑ Drama
- ❑ Jazz Band
- ❑ Music Theory
- ❑ Orchestra
- ❑ _____
- ❑ _____

Dual-Enrollment Courses:

- ❑ _____
- ❑ _____
- ❑ _____
- ❑ _____
- ❑ _____
- ❑ _____

Preparing For The Rest Of Your High School Courses

As we have gone through this workbook, there has been an obvious focus on your sophomore year. You will also need to begin to plan out the rest of your high school academic career. While looking at your sophomore year courses, take a few moments to start planning your junior year courses also. What does your 11th grade look like?

What questions do you have about your future classes?

1. _____

2. _____

3. _____

4. _____

5. _____

What extracurricular activities do you plan to participate in next year?

1. _____

2. _____

3. _____

4. _____

5. _____

Take your questions about your junior year courses to your high school counselor or graduation coach.

Social Media 101

Social media is the not-so-new reality of life for you as a high school student. It is a unique way to connect with family, friends, businesses, and colleges. However, it can also be detrimental if used improperly. I'm sure you can think of many examples of students and adult professionals really messing up when it comes to social media. Can you remember a celebrity's tweet that had to be deleted, or an individual stating that they were "hacked" after an offensive rant? You don't want to be the person that loses out on opportunities because of your online behavior.

Did you know that a majority of colleges and job recruiters research applicants' social media platforms as part of their review process? Institutions and businesses are looking at the whole person, and they want people who can represent their organization well.

I want you to enjoy your social media experience. However, here are some tips and suggestions to remember when it comes to your social media presence:

1. **Everything is public**: Today, it doesn't take the most sophisticated computer scientist to find out what you have been up to on the internet. Just because you deleted a post doesn't mean it's gone. Everything you post on the internet is traceable, yes EVERYTHING! The websites you visit, the music you download, and the online purchases you make can all be linked back to you. You leave a digital footprint everywhere you go on the World Wide Web. Just remember this when you are about to make that controversial post.

2. **Don't make emotional posts**: If you run to social media to vent every time something happens, stop it! One of the most common mistakes individuals make is posting on social media when they are mad or frustrated. Going to social media at an emotional time is a classic way to put your foot in your mouth. People have been fired for aggressively criticising their supervisor or badmouthing customers on their personal social media platforms. When you're emotional, you aren't thinking correctly, and apologies are likely to follow.

3. **Profile names precede your reputation**: Usually, you hear that your reputation precedes you. In other words, many people will hear something about you (positive or negative) before they actually meet you. In the case of social media, your profile name is your first impression. Controversial or offensive profile names will give viewers their first idea of who you are. Take a little time to think of what your profile name is saying about you.

4. **Don't post someone without their permission**: It is very important to respect someone's right to privacy. If they are not actively participating in your post, consider how they would feel if they were uploaded online. You would want someone to consider your rights as well.

5. **Don't embarrass your family**: For a majority of people, their family is their largest support group. For others, it may be anyone who has invested themselves into your success. They too, are now family. One of my strongest suggestions is not to publicly embarrass yourself and your family. Once it's out there, it's out there! When you do something stupid, some of the first questions will be about your family structure or upbringing. People will research who is associated with you, and why they let you do whatever you did. Yes, you do have free speech in the U.S. However, that just gives you the right to say it. It does not protect you from consequences once you say it. I'm pretty sure it won't take you long to think of several examples of people embarrassing themselves on social media.

6. **Talking to strangers is unsafe**: I know this seems pretty obvious, and you are old enough to manage your own social media platforms. However, if you watch the local news long enough, you will see a story about some student, or adult, who was abducted by someone they met online. I don't want you to be in this situation. There are some dangerous people out there that don't have your best interest at heart. Never give out your personal information, including where you are located.

7. **Routinely scrub your old posts**: Although someone could find deleted posts with a little time and motivation, it would be very helpful to get into the habit of reviewing your old posts periodically. Some posts don't paint you in the best light and just need to be deleted over time. Take the time to go over your posts to determine what may need to be removed to ensure you are sending the correct messages to the world.

8. **Proofread your posts**: You may or may not be surprised, but many students don't know how to spell. You don't want to look ignorant or uneducated on the World Wide Web. Take the time to look over your post before clicking that button to send to the social media universe.

9. **Be careful about what you share**: A lot of times, a funny video or meme is the joke we needed to keep our day going. However, a lot of high school students are obsessed with fighting videos laid with vulgarities. Remember, even though it's not your video or content, you are condoning it by having it associated with your account.

10. **Follow your top colleges**: Now, something I do want you to do on your social media: follow the social media platforms for your top college choices. This can be a great way to informally connect with them and learn about upcoming events. Tag them in posts about your accomplishments and aspirations to attend. Use your posts as a way to build your brand and increase their interest in accepting you.

Can you identify any of the social media mistakes with people you know? If so, which ones?

1. _____

2. _____

3. _____

4. _____

5. _____

What are some other good uses for social media?

1. _____

2. _____

3. _____

4. _____

Student Notes

_____

_____

_____

_____

_____

_____

_____

_____

_____

_____

_____

_____

_____

_____

_____

_____

CHAPTER 2

WHAT YOU SHOULD KNOW ABOUT COLLEGE

A college education is statistically your best chance for a financially stable future. However, a college education isn't the best option or fit for everyone. Some students will pursue a career in the military, or find a job in a trade. There are many success stories of athletes, musicians, and entrepreneurs who do very well for themselves without a college education. But chances are, if you do not educate yourself or develop a formal skill beyond high school, you will fall behind financially.

Post-secondary education doesn't always mean you have to attend a large college in your state. There are many options to further your education after high school. We will discuss those options in more detail later in the workbook.

In an average lifetime, someone with a college degree will earn over 1 million dollars more than someone with only a high school diploma (*http://usgovinfo.about.com/od/moneymatters/a/edandearnings.htm*). Long gone are the days where individuals can advance in companies with experience alone. Employers are looking for some type of educational completion that can demonstrate that you can commit to the rigors of a standard educational experience. Put simply, they want to know that you have both the intellect and the discipline to get a degree or certification. Additionally, as you move up in your professional career, you will see more and more individuals with graduate degrees, professional certifications, and specialized trainings beyond the Associate or Bachelor's degree level. You will see that there is a true correlation between education and income.

The good thing about your college experience is that it is going to be the best period of your life. When you aren't in class or studying, you will have lots of fun meeting new people, taking road trips, and learning more about yourself as a person.

What are some ideas you have about what college will be like?

1. _____

2. _____

3. _____

4. _____

5. _____

Understanding How Colleges Work

Although a college is an institution of higher learning, it is also a business! The purpose of a college is to educate young (and sometimes not so young) minds. It can be a gateway to entry into the workforce. It may inspire entrepreneurs to create products and jobs. It can enable individuals to discover their talent niche.

Therefore, it is you — "the customer, the student"— that is the driving financial force of a college. Your hard work, tuition, and success will essentially open doors for students coming behind you. Through your attendance and tuition dollars, a college can generate funds to pay faculty and staff, build new academic buildings and dorms, and create new experiences for future students.

You need to make your college decision a business decision. As you mature through high school, you will develop an idea of what type of college you want to attend based on the experience you are looking for. We will soon discuss the different types of colleges. I want you to go ahead and start thinking about what these institutions have to offer you, and whether it is a wise investment of your time and money there.

With proper planning, admissions into, and successful matriculation through, a college will be much easier.

Deal Breakers: What are some things that will prevent you from attending a particular college?

1. _____

2. _____

3. _____

Must Haves: What are some things a college needs to provide for you to attend?

1. _____

2. _____

3. _____

Types of Colleges

When trying to decide which college to attend, the first thing to think about is the type of colleges you have to choose from. There are many types of institutions of higher learning in the United States. They are designed for various types of students, who have varying needs, and are interested in a variety of programs of study. Understanding the type of college that you would like to attend is very important in narrowing down your college options. Although some colleges will fall into several different categories, here's a common explanation of the different types of institutions of higher education:

The Ivy Leagues

"Ivy League" is a trademarked name, representing a specific consortium or group of colleges and universities. There are 8 Ivy League institutions. Most people consider them to be America's top institutions. The term Ivy League is associated with prestige, academic excellence, selectivity in admissions, and social elitism. Many renowned U.S. leaders, business leaders, scientists, politicians, and lawyers received their degrees from Ivy League schools.

*Brown University, Columbia University, Cornell University, Dartmouth College
Harvard University, University of Pennsylvania, Princeton University, Yale University*

Source: http://collegeapps.about.com/od/choosingacollege/tp/ivy-league-schools.htm

Research Universities

Some of the world's most famous discoveries have been made through university research, including the origination of the internet, the discovery of the AIDS virus, and current advances in stem cell research. Research universities are generally larger, and often more prominent, institutions that have quite a few faculty members leading major research in their field.

Source: http://www.bestcollegereviews.org/top-research-universities/

Liberal Arts Colleges

Generally, liberal arts colleges emphasize undergraduate education only, and award at least half of their degrees in the liberal arts field of study. Liberal arts colleges focus on providing a broad general knowledge and developing general intellectual capacities, instead of faculty-led research.

Regional Universities and Colleges

These institutions can offer a full range of undergraduate and **graduate** level degree programs. They can even offer a few doctoral programs as well. They are called regional universities because they focus on the major needs of the region in which they are located.

Source: http://colleges.usnews.rankingsandreviews.com/best-colleges/rankings/regional-universities/top-public

State Universities or Colleges

These institutions are owned and run by one of the states as a part of the state's education system. State schools are considered public schools and can vary in terms of program and degree offerings.

Two-Year Colleges

These institutions are commonly known as a junior colleges or community colleges. These institutions generally offer Associate degrees and non-degree/diploma programs. Often, students can begin at a two-year college and transfer to a four-year college or university after he or she completes **core courses** or an Associate degree.

Private Colleges & Universities

These institutions are identified as independent schools that establish their own policies and goals, and do not depend on governmental funds to operate. Private institutions can be top elite schools or very small career-focused schools. Generally, private schools have higher tuition rates than state public schools.

Source: http://colleges.usnews.rankingsandreviews.com/best-colleges/rankings/undergrad-research-programs

HBCU's

Before the Civil War, higher education for African Americans was virtually non-existent. During the aftermath of the Civil War, a new population of free African American citizens were looking to further their education. Institutions were founded with the intention of serving African Americans.

These institutions have been deemed Historically Black Colleges & Universities, or HBCU's. A lot of HBCU's can trace their origin to a church or house, and most are located in the former slave states. Although HBCU is an identifier of an institution's culture and history, they can be placed in many different categories including public, private, four-year institutions, medical and law schools.

http://www.collegeview.com/articles/article/the-history-of-historically-black-colleges-and-universties

Technical Colleges

Technical colleges, formally known as vocational schools, are institutions that allow students to earn a degree, diploma, or certification in a trade. The purpose of a technical college is to get students out into the workforce quickly. Technical colleges generally have a service area or region, and do not recruit students in another technical college's area.

For-Profit Institutions

For-profit institutions, also known as proprietary institutions, differ from traditional state schools because they are owned and operated by a private, profit-seeking business. Although some for-profit institutions offer degrees, a lot will offer diplomas or certificates in different career fields. The tuition will generally be higher in these institutions. However, there is some attraction for some students to attend a for-profit institution, including a shortened length of program and career-focused courses.

Now that you know the common types of colleges, start thinking about which type of college will allow you to be successful based on your needs. Choosing the type of college you would like to attend can be tricky. Many students have been taught that some schools are better than others. This concept only applies if you know what your end goal will be.

One thing I want you to keep in mind is that every student isn't going to a 4-year college. Furthermore, a Bachelor's degree isn't the best option for each student. You will need to determine which option is best for you. As you can see in the above section, there are many opportunities to attain a higher education.

I have worked in state, technical, and for profit colleges. At this time, I have colleagues with Master's degrees making less money than students who I assisted in graduating from technical colleges. My point is that you have to be strategic in your planning. The type of college, programs of study offered, and resources that it provides should all be factors in your college selection process.

What types of colleges are you interested in, and why?

1. _____

Why: _____

_____

2. _____

Why: _____

_____

3. _____

Why: _____

_____

4. _____

Why: _____

_____

Community Service, Leadership & Involvement

Colleges are looking for well-rounded students to become leaders and to be the face of the institution. Yes, you can be accepted into a college with just your academic aptitude. However, if it comes down to accepting you or another student with the same GPA and test scores, the tie-breaker is usually the student's involvement in extracurricular activities.

Take advantage of the easy access to organizations and teams that you can associate yourself with in high school, church, and in your community. Play a leadership role in the organization, start a community project, or apply for a great summer internship. Find ways to make yourself stand out to admissions departments.

Here are a couple examples of ways to donate your time:

1. Search for volunteer match opportunities in your area.

2. Research the United Way to see what types of volunteer activities or organizations they have available to high school students.

3. The Scouts are great organizations to be a part of, and they give scholarships.

4. Contact your local Boys & Girls Club to mentor a younger student, or research how to become a Big Brother or Big Sister.

5. Get a group of your friends together and donate your time to building a house with Habitat for Humanity.

6. Consider volunteering your time at the local elementary or middle school by helping students with their homework.

7. Donate some time at a nursing home. You can read to, or sit with, some of the seniors. You might learn a thing or two.

8. If you are not an athlete, but interested in participating in a sports program… become a team manager or score keeper.

If these types of projects don't interest you, create your own. Put together an event to increase awareness of a topic, raise money, collect items for the needy, or find a way to bring the community together.

List some community service activities you <u>will</u> participate in this year.

Organization 1: _____

Potential Activity 1: _____

Potential Activity 2: _____

Potential Activity 3: _____

Organization 2: _____

Potential Activity 1: _____

Potential Activity 2: _____

Potential Activity 3: _____

Organization 3: _____

Potential Activity 1: _____

Potential Activity 2: _____

Potential Activity 3: _____

Student Notes

CHAPTER 3

PAYING FOR A COLLEGE EDUCATION

The financial aid process can seem intimidating for students and parents. However, it doesn't have to be. Use this section to gain an understanding of how you can explore multiple options for funding a college education.

The first thing I want you to understand is that you have to consider more than just **tuition** when thinking about paying for a college education. Although tuition is one of the major factors in your college selection process, there is an entire **cost of attendance** that you will need to think about. The cost of attendance will be different at each college.

The cost of attendance is comprised of the following, each academic year:

1. **Tuition & Fees**: Along with comparing the tuition of a college, you should also compare the fees that are associated as well. Some colleges will have more fees than others. Common fees at colleges are: Activity, Athletic, Library, Parking, and Technology fees. Research your top college choices to see all the mandatory fees that you will have to pay.

2. **Books & Supplies**: College courses require textbooks or eBooks, and they can get pretty expensive. Most students will get their books from the college's bookstore. However, if the bookstore prices get too expensive, you might have to seek other options to receive your books at a lower price.

3. **Room & Board**: While at college, you will have to reside somewhere. Most students will live on campus in one of the dormitory options. Compare the costs of the dorms at different colleges to see who has the lowest price. The colleges will have different dorm styles as well. The dorms are a must-see when going on your college tours. The other living options to consider are off-campus alternatives, such as an apartment or

rented house. You may also consider living at home if your college is close enough. If it works out for your family, living at home may be a great way to save money in the long run. Also, included in room & board are meal plans. Each college will have different levels and options of meal plans for you to choose from. Some colleges have cafeterias only. Others may have alternate food courts and coffee shops that you may have access to. Find out which one will be best for you.

4. **Transportation**: Depending on where you attend college, transportation can be a major financial factor. Your ability to get back and forth from college should be considered in the financial decision-making process of your college selection. Will you be at a college that allows a freshman to have a car? Does the college have a campus bus system? Is there a bus that can take you from campus to the store? Will you need to travel back home by car, bus, or plane?

5. **Personal Expenses**: The personal expenses of students may vary, but everyone will need to consider the cost of the things needed to live away from home. The items needed to move into your dorm, clothes, and other expenses should be considered.

Research your top colleges to determine what their cost of attendance will be. You should be able to find this information on their websites. If not, make a quick call to their admissions department.

What is the cost of attendance for your top colleges?

1. _____ COA: _____

2. _____ COA: _____

3. _____ COA: _____

4. _____ COA: _____

5. _____ COA: _____

Understanding Financial Aid

In most cases, the cost of a college and the **financial aid options** are the top determining factors if a student will attend a certain college. Simply put, financial aid is funds provided to students and families to help pay for a college education. It can come from several sources:

1. The Federal Government

    The federal government is the largest provider of higher education funding for students.

2. The State Government

    Most states have some type of educational funding offered to students who graduate from high school in their state. These funds could come from state taxes, lottery, or other funding options from the state. Research your state to see if there are funds available to you.

3. Your College

    Colleges also provide funding specific to students who attend the college. These scholarship and fellowship opportunities are called institutional funding because it's coming from that particular institution.

4. A Non-Profit or Private Organization/Business

    Private organizations also offer funding for students to attend college. When researching scholarship opportunities, students will see scholarships from large companies like Coke-a-Cola, Home Depot, and Bank of America. Scholarships are also available from civic or community organizations like the Boys & Girls Club, Alumni Greek Letter Organizations, or The United Negro College Fund.

The Office of Federal Student Aid provides over $150 billion in federal grants, loans, and work-study funds each year. This office also developed the Free Application for Federal Student Aid, commonly known as the **FAFSA**, and processes over 22 million application submissions yearly.

At this time, I just want you to be aware of the application. You and your parents won't apply for financial aid until your senior year in high school.

What are some specific ways you plan to pay for your college education?

1. _____

   How: _____

   _____

2. _____

   How: _____

   _____

3. _____

   How: _____

   _____

4. _____

   How: _____

   _____

Military As An Option for Education

All students are not going to go straight to college out of high school. Some will get jobs in a trade and others will join one of the branches of the U.S. Armed Services… and that can be a great thing!

Sometimes students and their parents aren't familiar with the potential benefits of joining one of the five military branches:

United States Army   **United States Marine Corps**   **United States Navy**

United States Air Force   **United States Coast Guard**

The military will be a great opportunity for some students and families. Here are some benefits of becoming a member of the U.S Military:

1. **Allows you to serve our country**: Serving in the U.S. Military is an honor, and is given the utmost respect. These individuals protect our country and all citizens within. Some students will feel a duty to join a branch.

2. **Allows you to see the world**: As a member of the military, you may have the opportunity to see many places in the world that civilians will have to pay considerable money to see.

3. **Gives structure for those who need it**: Some students will need the structure that only the military can provide. Discipline, character and teamwork are key pillars of the military lifestyle.

4. **Earn money while others are in college**: Joining the military means you have a job! It is a great way to start your career.

5. **Specialized professional experience**: There are many career fields that require high levels of security clearance that will be great choices to pursue. Also, you will have opportunities to continually educate yourself in your chosen profession.

6. **Pay for your college education**: As a member of the military, you are eligible for tuition assistance for your service. Sometimes, you can transfer your educational benefits to your children when it's time for them to go to college.

7. **Veteran's benefits after serving**: In addition to the educational benefits, former service members receive many benefits, including priority for a lot of civilian jobs, assistance with home buying, free or low cost medical expenses, and numerous discounts and incentive programs.

8. **There are part-time options:** You will have the option to also choose from part-time military options through the Reserves and National Guard.

If you are potentially interested in pursuing the military as an option, talk with your counselor or ROTC department to see when they will invite military recruiters to speak to students. Research the **ASVAB** test to see what type of career you would be successful at in the military. They have most of the same jobs that students will pursue in the civilian sector (Nursing, Management, Computer Science, Law Enforcement, etc.) Also, the military can be a great option for higher pay if you enlist as an officer after you graduate from college!

State Funding Opportunities

Many states also have financial aid opportunities for students who graduate from high school within the state. It is generally used to incentivize students to attend the in-state colleges, instead of leaving the state to pursue a higher education. This is important to state lawmakers because when students attend in-state colleges, it helps the economy of that state. How, you may ask? When students pay tuition at a college, either through loans or out-of-pocket, they are keeping the money in that state. Most college students will also work in their home state after they graduate. With that much money potentially leaving the state through students interested in attending college in other states, lawmakers want to encourage students to keep their tuition dollars right at home.

State financial aid programs are funded through the state lottery, taxes, or other means. There may be scholarship or grant opportunities to assists students with college tuition. A student's eligibility is usually based on his/her merit-worthiness (GPA, test scores, etc.) Generally, students will need to complete the FAFSA and/or a state application to start the process to receive state funds.

Here are a few examples of state funding opportunities for high school students around the country:

- Florida: Bright Futures Program (Florida Medallion Scholars Award)

- Georgia: HOPE Scholarship (Helping Outstanding Pupils Educationally)

- Kentucky KEES Program (Kentucky Educational Excellence Scholarship)

- Tennessee TELS Program (Tennessee Education Lottery Scholarship)

- South Carolina: LIFE Program (Legislative Incentives for Future Excellence)

- West Virginia: PROMISE (Providing Real Opportunities for Maximizing In-State Student Excellence)

You will need to do some research and speak to your counselor to learn about the funding opportunities that your state offers and the qualifications you must meet to be eligible. Since I live in Georgia, here are a few examples of the programs in my state:

1. **The HOPE Scholarship:** Helping Outstanding Pupils Educationally, or HOPE Scholarship program, is available for students that have demonstrated academic achievement and are seeking a college degree. There are several ways to become eligible for the HOPE Scholarship, either by graduating from high school as a HOPE Scholar or by earning it while in college.

2. **HOPE Grant:** The HOPE Grant program is available for students seeking a technical certificate or diploma, in specific programs of study.

Are there state funding options where you live?   ☐ Yes   ☐ No

Program 1 Name: _____

Information: _____

_____

_____

_____

Requirement 1: _____

Requirement 2: _____

Program 2 Name: _____

Information: _____

_____

_____

_____

Requirement 1: _____

Requirement 2: _____

Scholarships 101

When it comes to funding a college education, everybody wants scholarships! However, with all of the money that's out there… a lot of students still won't get one. Sometimes they don't meet the established criteria for the scholarship award. Others won't put in the work to do the research and essays. Many students just may not know about them. It is incumbent upon you, the student, to seek out and apply for scholarship opportunities. Scholarships can fall into a few different categories:

Academic Scholarships are awarded to those students that have done the hard work needed for colleges to reward their academic efforts.

Athletic Scholarships are given to student-athletes that have put in the hard work to be noticed by an athletic department.

Institutional Scholarships are those scholarships that are given from the college. They do not transfer to other colleges. Example: An athlete who earns a scholarship to play football at the University of Georgia cannot transfer his UGA scholarship to Georgia Tech if he wants to transfer.

National Scholarships are scholarships that students from all over the country will compete for. They can come from a private company, a wealthy family trust or foundation, a national civic or community organization, etc.

Merit-based Scholarships are scholarships that are earned through good grades, high test scores, etc. with no attachment to household financial status. Rich and poor students can qualify for merit-based scholarships because it is based on their performance.

Need-Based Scholarships are scholarships that are given to students who want to attend college, but don't have the household financial resources to pay for a college education. These students will still want to have a competitive student profile. Students who have a high household financial status generally are not eligible for need-based scholarships.

You will need to put yourself in the best position possible to receive a scholarship. Every year, we hear about a student who receives an enormous amount of scholarship funds to pay for their college education. That doesn't happen by accident! These students put in the hard work to be successful. This can also be you. Your first step is to make sure you are scholarship-worthy or what I call a "hot commodity" student.

1. Work to get the highest GPA you can.

2. Prepare to score highly on standardized tests.

3. Get involved in leadership roles, sports teams, and community service.

4. Have a story to tell. Do something/have an experience worth sharing.

5. <u>Write</u> the essays <u>Right</u>.

6. Do your research. The money will not come to you!

7. Apply to as many scholarships as possible.

List scholarships that you can apply for during your sophomore year.

1. _____ Amount: _____

2. _____ Amount: _____

3. _____ Amount: _____

4. _____ Amount: _____

5. _____ Amount: _____

6. _____ Amount: _____

7. _____ Amount: _____

8. _____ Amount: _____

9. _____ Amount: _____

10. _____ Amount: _____

Student Notes

CHAPTER 4

CONNECTING YOUR PROGRAM TO A CAREER

While at your institution of higher education, be it a 4-year, 2-year, technical college, etc. you will take courses in your field of study. The point of the going to school is to put yourself in a better position to land a high paying job.

Many students will pursue programs of study, and subsequently a career, based on what they see around them. How many of your friends are interested in a job that one of their parents or family member does? Are you interested in a position because your parents are in the field? The unfortunate reality is that there are thousands of untapped career options that students could be exposed to, if they just did a little research. Take the time to complete a career assessment to take to help you understand what careers might be a good fit for who you are.

Also, when thinking about a career option, remember that there are many positions within that career. Take a career in Movie Production for example. How many positions can you identify in this field?

Production Professionals

1. _____

2. _____

3. _____

4. _____

5. _____

6. _____

7. _____

8. _____

9. _____

10. _____

Now, let's try it to get a little deeper. When choosing your career, not only do you have to think of multiple positions in the field, you also have to consider day-to-day responsibilities and salary. Take couple of minutes to research a few other career fields. This time, try to think of some positions that aren't so obvious. For example, the obvious choice for law would be a lawyer or a judge. Let's see what other positions you can find.

Research and list some "not so obvious" positions that fall within these careers.

Law:

Position 1: _____ Salary: _____ per/year

Responsibility: _____

Position 2: _____ Salary: _____ per/year

Responsibility: _____

Position 3: _____ Salary: _____ per/year

Responsibility: _____

Transportation:

Position 1: _____ Salary: _____ per/year

Responsibility: _____

Position 2: _____ Salary: _____ per/year

Responsibility: _____

Position 3: _____ Salary: _____ per/year

Responsibility: _____

Healthcare:

Position 1: _____ Salary: _____ per/year

Responsibility: _____

Position 2: _____ Salary: _____ per/year

Responsibility: _____

Position 3: _____ Salary: _____ per/year

Responsibility: _____

High Demand Careers

The next step in the career selection process is to identify the potential availability of careers in your area. Some positions are needed in regional areas in the country. Here are a few examples: (1) ice road truckers really aren't needed in Miami, Florida., and (2) deep water fisherman really aren't needed in Omaha, Nebraska. However, there are some jobs that all states need and some states may need a certain type of job more than others. This difference determines the demand of a certain career. There are some careers that are considered high demand. They are considered high demand careers for two reasons:

1. generally, there is a high need for the position in an area, or state; and

2. in many instances, these careers have more jobs opportunities than qualified candidates.

Take a few moments to research a few careers that are considered in high demand in your area. You can find this information on your state's Department of Labor website, or by an online search of high demand careers in your state.

Position 1: _____ Salary: _____ per/year

Responsibility: _____

Position 2: _____ Salary: _____ per/year

Responsibility: _____

Position 3: _____ Salary: _____ per/year

Responsibility: _____

Position 4: _____ Salary: _____ per/year

Responsibility: _____

Position 5: _____ Salary: _____ per/year

Responsibility: _____

Would you consider any of these high demand careers in your area? ☐ Yes   ☐ No

What Is S.T.E.M.?

In recent years, there has been a major push for careers in the S.T.E.M. fields. S.T.E.M. stands for Science, Technology, Engineering, and Mathematics. The U.S. is looking for talented young professionals to fill important science-based positions. There are many high paying jobs for those who want to pursue careers in these fields.

Common Science Careers

- Biologist
- Chemist
- Dietician & Nutritionist
- Environment Scientist
- Forensic Biologist
- Geneticist
- Medical Scientist

Common Technology Careers

- Application Developer
- Computer & Information Systems Manager
- Cybersecurity Analyst
- Database Administrator
- Software Developer
- Web Developer

Common Engineering Careers

- Aerospace Engineer
- Biomedical Engineer
- Chemical Engineer
- Civil Engineer
- Computer Engineer

Common Mathematics Careers

- Actuary Scientist
- Financial Analyst
- Mathematician
- Statistician

What are a few other S.T.E.M. careers can you think of?

1. _____

2. _____

3. _____

4. _____

5. _____

Does Salary Affect Your Household?

Yes, your salary absolutely affects your household. The simple example is that those with higher salaries acquire more things than those who have a lower salary. However, a salary isn't the only aspect of a job to consider when choosing your career. You also want to look at benefits, perks and work-life balance. Here are a few examples:

1. Teacher: They have to contend with the challenge of reaching a variety of students, strenuous testing requirements, and often have to take work home. However, they also receive summers and other breaks off. Would you consider a job in education?

2. Nurse: Depending on the type of nurse, they often work around sick individuals; they have to be ok with blood and emergency situations, and may possibly be required to clean up human bodily fluids. However, most nurses only work three days per week. Knowing this, would you consider a job in nursing?

3. Entrepreneur: Business owners have a lot of work to do. They play the roles of the sales, marketing, shipping, quality control, purchaser, customer service, etc. However, they get to make their own schedule and usually only answer to themselves. Would you be interested in owning your own business?

If you can narrow down your prospective career options, you can begin to research what type of salary you might expect. However, remember that no matter what your salary may be, you will have to learn how to budget with what you are given.

What are some benefits you would want your career to have?

1. _____

2. _____

3. _____

4. _____

5. _____

Student Career Questionnaire
(No research required)

Please answer the questions below based on your current plans after college graduation. Once you complete the questions, input your budgetary answers in the "Your Projection" sections of the Monthly Budget Activity Sheet.

What job position do you want after you graduate from college? _____

What will your residence look like? ❑ 1 Bedroom Apartment   ❑ 2 Bedroom Apartment

❑ 3 Bedroom Apartment   ❑ Condo   ❑ Townhouse   ❑ Single Family Home

Where will you be located? City: _____, State: _____

How will it be furnished?   ❑ Brand New Furniture   ❑ Pre-Owned Furniture

❑   Discount Mall Furniture

What car do you want? Year: _____, Make: _____, Model: _____

What type of cell phone will you have? Make: _____, Model: _____

Would you like to get a new phone each year?   ❑ Yes   ❑ No

Do you plan to go clothes/shoes shopping each month?   ❑ Yes   ❑ No

Do you plan to hang out socially with your friends/significant other?   ❑ Yes   ❑ No

Do you plan to purchase nice electronics (computer, TV, tablets, etc.)?   ❑ Yes   ❑ No

Do you plan to take several vacation trips each year?   ❑ Yes   ❑ No

Do you plan to have a pet?   ❑ Yes   ❑ No

Monthly Budget Questionnaire
(Research required)

At this time, we need to quantify (connect numbers to) your plan. This is how you will be able to understand what money management is all about. I want you to do this in a real life scenario. Please research the following aspects of your plans and input your researched answer in the "After Research" sections of the Monthly Budget Activity Sheet. Without knowing your current state of residence and the appropriate tax percentages, we'll make it easy by not considering taxes in this exercise. However, please keep in mind that the numbers we discover through this exercise will likely be lower in the real world due to taxes.

What is the entry level position for your career called? _____

- *Ex. If you want to be a Criminal Investigator, the entry level position may be called Investigator 1.*

What is the <u>local</u> salary range for <u>entry level</u> positions in your career field? _____ - _____ / year

- *Take the median of the range and divide it by 12. If the annual salary range is $40,000 - $50,000 for this position in your city, take $45,000 and divide it by 12. This will give you your monthly income before taxes.*

What is the average local rent/mortgage for the housing option you chose? _____/ month

- *Research some of the apartment complexes, condos, houses, etc. and determine what the average payment will be in your local area.*

What is the cost of the year, make, and model of the car you selected? _____/ month

- *To determine the monthly payment, search for a car payment calculator. Input the cost of your car, for a 5 year or 60-month term, at a 3% interest rate. Your real interest rate will be determined by you credit score.*

What is the average cost of the insurance for the year, make, and model of the car you selected? _____/ month.

- *Search for the average insurance cost for your car. If you have difficulty getting an average, ask your parents or trusted adult how much their car insurance costs them each month.*

How much will you have to spend on each utility bill or other household expenses?

- *Talk to your parents or trusted adult to get an idea of the expenses associated with the bills.*

How much do you want to put away for savings and retirement each month? _____ (S), _____ (R)

- *Saving money for a rainy day is very important. How much do you want to invest in your future?*

Most employees receive healthcare from their job. How much you do think healthcare will be? _____/ month

- *Talk to your parents or trusted adult to get an idea of how much healthcare is costing them.*

How much are you going to spend on entertainment, going out, dating, etc.? _____/ month

Now that you have done the research on your local area, let's see how you fair on a monthly budget.

Monthly Budget Activity

Income	Your Projection	After Research
Monthly Salary	$	$
Other	$	$
Other	$	$

Savings		
Savings	Your Projection	After Research
IRA/Retirement	$	$
Savings Account	$	$

Housing Expenses		
Expense	Your Projection	After Research
Rent/Mortgage	$	$
Insurance	$	$
Home Repair	$	$
Other	$	$

Transportation		
Expense	Your Projection	After Research
Car Payment	$	$
Car Insurance	$	$
Maintenance/Repair	$	$
Gasoline/Electricity	$	$

Personal Debt		
Expense	Your Projection	After Research
Credit Cards	$	$
Student Loans	$	$
Other	$	$

Food		
Expense	Your Projection	After Research
Groceries	$	$
Eating Out	$	$

Healthcare		
Expense	Your Projection	After Research
Doctor/Dentist	$	$
Health Insurance	$	$
Health Products	$	$

Entertainment		
Expense	Your Projection	After Research
Events/Movies/etc.	$	$
Other	$	$

Miscellaneous Expenses		
Expense	Your Projection	After Research
	$	$
	$	$

Utility/Household Bills		
Expense	Your Projection	After Research
Electric/Power Bill	$	$
Cable/TV/Internet	$	$
Cell Phone	$	$
Water Bill	$	$
Subscriptions	$	$
Other	$	$

Researched Total Income – Total Expense			
Income	_	Expenses	Balance
$	_	$	$

Hopefully, going through this exercise has shown you just how fast money is accounted for. Now, based on the information from the budget above, where do you see that you can make some changes to your household income and expenses?

Where do you see that you will need to make some changes?

1. _____

2. _____

3. _____

4. _____

5. _____

Student Notes

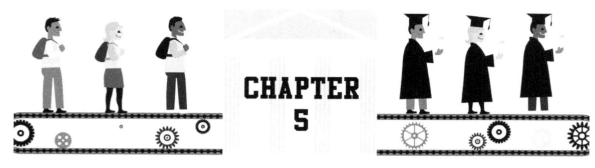

CHAPTER 5

SOPHOMORE RESOURCES & TOOLS

The Sophomore Resources & Tools section is designed to provide sophomore students with some helpful documents to be used throughout the college readiness process this year. Use the tools provided in this section to ensure that you have identified and covered all aspects of your college readiness plan. Included in the Student Tools section:

- State High School Graduation Requirements

- Sophomore Year Checklist

- Student Brag Sheet

- General Standardized Test Taking Tips

- Community Service Log

- Student Study Skills

- Projected Junior Year Classes

- Projected Senior Year Classes

State High School Graduation Requirements

Your state requires how many credits/units to be a:

Sophomore: _____ Junior: _____ Senior: _____ Graduate: _____

Units of English: _____
Specific Classes:
- ❑ _____
- ❑ _____
- ❑ _____
- ❑ _____

Units of Math: _____
Specific Classes:
- ❑ _____
- ❑ _____
- ❑ _____
- ❑ _____

Units of Science: _____
Specific Classes:
- ❑ _____
- ❑ _____
- ❑ _____
- ❑ _____

Units of Social Studies: _____
Specific Classes:
- ❑ _____
- ❑ _____
- ❑ _____
- ❑ _____

Units of Health & PE: _____
Specific Classes:
- ❑ _____
- ❑ _____
- ❑ _____
- ❑ _____

Units of CTAE: _____
Specific Classes:
- ❑ _____
- ❑ _____
- ❑ _____
- ❑ _____

Units of Foreign Lang: _____
Specific Classes:
- ❑ _____
- ❑ _____
- ❑ _____
- ❑ _____

Units of Fine Arts: _____
Specific Classes:
- ❑ _____
- ❑ _____
- ❑ _____
- ❑ _____

Units of Electives: _____
Specific Classes:
- ❑ _____
- ❑ _____
- ❑ _____
- ❑ _____

Notes:

_____

_____

_____

_____

Sophomore Year Checklist

❑ Continue building a relationship with your high school counselor, or introduce yourself to your new one.

❑ Focus on your grades. Get the best grades you can this year. Get a tutor if needed.

❑ Talk to your counselor about Honors, Advanced Placement, and Dual Enrollment courses, if interested.

❑ Set some goals for your junior and senior years. Talk to your counselor, parents, and teachers about them.

❑ Attend events that the counseling department hosts and try to get your parents to come.

❑ Consider joining additional clubs and organizations.

❑ Increase your participation in community service activities.

❑ _____

❑ _____

❑ _____

❑ _____

❑ _____

❑ _____

❑ _____

Sophomore Student Brag Sheet

Honor Roll: ❏ Yes ❏ No

What do you consider to be your strongest personal asset? _____

3 adjectives that describe you:

1. _____

2. _____

3. _____

Potential Recommendation Letter Writers:

1. _____

2. _____

3. _____

Honors & AP Courses:

1. _____   _____   _____
   Course Name   *Academic Year*   *Grade/AP Test Score*

2. _____   _____   _____
   Course Name   *Academic Year*   *Grade/AP Test Score*

3. _____   _____   _____
   Course Name   *Academic Year*   *Grade/AP Test Score*

4. _____   _____   _____
   Course Name   *Academic Year*   *Grade/AP Test Score*

5. _____   _____   _____
   Course Name   *Academic Year*   *Grade/AP Test Score*

Academic/Athletic/Music Awards:

1. _____   _____
   Award   *Year*

2. _____   _____
   Award   *Year*

3. _____   _____
   Award   *Year*

School Related Clubs & Organizations:

1. _____   _____
   Club/Organization/Team   *Office/Position*

2. _____   _____
   Club/Organization/Team   *Office/Position*

3. _____   _____
   Club/Organization/Team   *Office/Position*

4. _____   _____
   Club/Organization/Team   *Office/Position*

5. _____   _____
   Club/Organization/Team   *Office/Position*

Non-School Related Clubs & Organizations:

1. _____   _____
   Club/Organization/Team   *Office/Position*

2. _____   _____
   Club/Organization/Team   *Office/Position*

3. _____   _____
   Club/Organization/Team   *Office/Position*

Volunteer/Community Service:

1. _____   _____
   Club/Organization/Team   *Office/Position*

2. _____   _____
   Club/Organization/Team   *Office/Position*

3. _____   _____
   Club/Organization/Team   *Office/Position*

Special Interests & Talents:

1. _____

2. _____

3. _____

What sets you apart from other students?

What accomplishments are you most proud of?

Personal Goals:

Academic Goals:

PSAT & ACT Information:

PSAT/SAT Scores

Date Taken: _____ Score: Reading: _____ Writing & Language: _____ Math: _____ Essay: _____

Total: _____

Date Taken: _____ Score: Reading: _____ Writing & Language: _____ Math: _____ Essay: _____

Total: _____

Date Taken: _____ Score: Reading: _____ Writing & Language: _____ Math: _____ Essay: _____

Total: _____

ACT Aspire/ACT Scores

Date Taken: _____ English: _____ Math: _____ Reading: _____ Science: _____ Writing: _____

Composite Score: _____

Date Taken: _____ English: _____ Math: _____ Reading: _____ Science: _____ Writing: _____

Composite Score: _____

Date Taken: _____ English: _____ Math: _____ Reading: _____ Science: _____ Writing: _____

Composite Score: _____

General Standardized Test Taking Tips

1. **Listen carefully to the instructions and follow the directions given to you.** Specifically follow the instructions that the exam proctor gives during the pre-test time. Make sure to fill in the form as directed, and always use a No. 2 pencil. Fill in answers completely and don't go ahead if permission is not given.

2. **Read Carefully.** This can be a difficult task as you progress through the test. To ensure that you have given the question the attention it needs and you don't make careless mistakes, consider all the options before selecting your answer.

3. **Answer the easy questions first.** Sometimes it is best to get the points that you can as early as you possible. Working on the easier questions first allows you to take your time on the more difficult questions later. It will prevent you from running out of time on questions you could have answered.

4. **Eliminate answer choices that you know are wrong.** Use logic and deductive reasoning to reduce your answer options. If you can get your options down to two potential answers you have greatly increased your chances of getting it right.

5. **Answer every question and make educated guesses.** Both the SAT and ACT scores are based on the questions you get right. Neither test will penalize you for guessing, so try to make an educated guess on the questions you just don't know about. Answering every question can only help you.

6. **Use your test booklet as scratch paper & keep your answer sheet neat.** The answer sheet is the most important document in this room. Make sure to do all of your scratch work in the test booklet only. If you need to change your answer, be sure to fully erase the previous bubble. You don't want to give a reason not to give you your points.

7. **Check your answer sheet regularly.** Continually check your spot between the test booklet and the answer sheet. It would be a tragedy if you got to the last answer row and realized all of your answers are off by one question. This is very important if you are skipping questions.

8. **Work at an even, steady pace and limit your time on any one question.** The test is designed for students to spend a certain amount of time on each question. Don't get caught up on one particular question. Skip it, and come back to it. Use your mental clock to tell yourself if you are moving too slowly. You don't want to run out of time. Conversely, you don't want to speed through the test either. That's when you make the careless mistakes.

Source: Collegeboard.com

Community Service Time Sheet Log

Colleges are looking for well-rounded students. Get involved in community service activities in your area. Use the community service time sheets to document your community service hours and activities.

Date	Organization	Community Service Tasks	Hours	Supervisor

Special Notes	Total Hours

Student Study Skills Tips

One of the most important things you can do to put yourself in a better position for success is to establish strong study skills. You will rely on these skills throughout your high school and college career. Some students can just pay attention in class to learn the material, while others have to put in a lot of extra study time to be successful. Here are a few tips that will assist you in creating your arsenal of study skills:

1. Improve your information intake abilities: Before you get to the studying part, you need to be in class to receive the initial information. Your ability to retain information is the foundation of study skills. You simply have to pay attention in class, as well as listen and read for understanding.

2. Create a note taking system that works for you: While in class, you will need to create a way to document important information that works best with your learning style. Do you rather take notes verbatim, or do you listen for the important information? Are you someone that likes to outline, or do you utilize simple bullet points?

3. Work with information multiple times: Many have said it takes someone to see something three times before they make a connection to it. Try it out for yourself. Review the information once. For the second round, write it down. On the third round, say it out aloud. When reviewing it three times, it should stick.

4. Study in short spurts: Studies have shown that students retain more information when they review it in short spurts of time with breaks in between. Try timing your study spurts in 20-minute increments with a 10-minute break in between.

5. Ask questions for clarity: If you come across information that you have questions about, be sure to discuss it with your teacher as soon as you can. You will need to switch the confusion to a confirmation so that you don't create a mental hiccup in your mind in reference to that particular piece of information. Have you ever experienced information where you never remember the correct way to do it when it comes up? That's a hiccup.

6. Get a good night's sleep: Everyone knows that it's a best practice to get a lot of rest the night before a big day. However, did you know two nights before the big day is when you need the most rest? Studies have shown that information transitions from short-term memory to long-term memory while you sleep. With a good night's sleep two nights prior, you will have a better experience during the big day.

Projected Junior Year Classes

English/Language Arts:

- ❑ American Literature
- ❑ British Literature
- ❑ Comparative Literature
- ❑ Composition
- ❑ Contemporary Literature
- ❑ Creative Writing
- ❑ Debate
- ❑ Journalism
- ❑ Poetry
- ❑ Rhetoric
- ❑ World Literature
- ❑ _____
- ❑ _____

Foreign Language:

- ❑ American Sign Language
- ❑ Arabic
- ❑ Chinese
- ❑ French
- ❑ German
- ❑ Italian
- ❑ Japanese
- ❑ Korean
- ❑ Latin
- ❑ Portuguese
- ❑ Russian
- ❑ Spanish
- ❑ _____
- ❑ _____

Honors or AP Courses:

- ❑ _____
- ❑ _____
- ❑ _____
- ❑ _____
- ❑ _____

Mathematics:

- ❑ Algebra 1
- ❑ Algebra 2
- ❑ Calculus
- ❑ Geometry
- ❑ Integrated Math
- ❑ Pre-Algebra
- ❑ Pre-Calculus
- ❑ Statistics
- ❑ Trigonometry
- ❑ _____
- ❑ _____

CTAE:

- ❑ Accounting
- ❑ Auto Repair
- ❑ Business
- ❑ Computer Science
- ❑ Cosmetology
- ❑ Culinary Arts
- ❑ Entrepreneurship
- ❑ Fashion Design
- ❑ Graphic Design
- ❑ Healthcare
- ❑ JROTC
- ❑ Law/Criminal Justice
- ❑ Marketing
- ❑ Music Production
- ❑ Nutrition
- ❑ Robotics
- ❑ Web Design
- ❑ Welding
- ❑ Wood Working
- ❑ _____
- ❑ _____

Science:

- ❑ Anatomy & Physiology
- ❑ Astronomy
- ❑ Biology
- ❑ Botany
- ❑ Chemistry
- ❑ Earth Science
- ❑ Environmental Science
- ❑ Forensic Science
- ❑ Life Science
- ❑ Oceanography
- ❑ Organic Chemistry
- ❑ Physical Science
- ❑ Physics
- ❑ Zoology
- ❑ _____
- ❑ _____

Physical Education:

- ❑ Aerobics
- ❑ Gymnastics
- ❑ Health
- ❑ Physical Education
- ❑ Swimming
- ❑ Wellness
- ❑ Weight Training
- ❑ _____
- ❑ _____

Visual Arts:

- ❑ Art
- ❑ Art History
- ❑ Digital Media
- ❑ Drawing
- ❑ Film Production/Video
- ❑ Photography
- ❑ _____
- ❑ _____

Social Studies:

- ❑ American History
- ❑ Anthropology
- ❑ Current Events
- ❑ Economics
- ❑ European History
- ❑ Geography
- ❑ International Relations
- ❑ Political Science
- ❑ Psychology
- ❑ Religious Studies
- ❑ Sociology
- ❑ US Government
- ❑ World History
- ❑ World Religions
- ❑ _____
- ❑ _____

Performing Arts:

- ❑ Choir
- ❑ Concert Band
- ❑ Dance
- ❑ Drama
- ❑ Jazz Band
- ❑ Music Theory
- ❑ Orchestra
- ❑ _____
- ❑ _____

Dual-Enrollment Courses:

- ❑ _____
- ❑ _____
- ❑ _____
- ❑ _____
- ❑ _____
- ❑ _____

Projected Senior Year Classes

English/Language Arts:

- ☐ American Literature
- ☐ British Literature
- ☐ Comparative Literature
- ☐ Composition
- ☐ Contemporary Literature
- ☐ Creative Writing
- ☐ Debate
- ☐ Journalism
- ☐ Poetry
- ☐ Rhetoric
- ☐ World Literature
- ☐ _____
- ☐ _____

Foreign Language:

- ☐ American Sign Language
- ☐ Arabic
- ☐ Chinese
- ☐ French
- ☐ German
- ☐ Italian
- ☐ Japanese
- ☐ Korean
- ☐ Latin
- ☐ Portuguese
- ☐ Russian
- ☐ Spanish
- ☐ _____
- ☐ _____

Honors or AP Courses:

- ☐ _____
- ☐ _____
- ☐ _____
- ☐ _____
- ☐ _____

Mathematics:

- ☐ Algebra 1
- ☐ Algebra 2
- ☐ Calculus
- ☐ Geometry
- ☐ Integrated Math
- ☐ Pre-Algebra
- ☐ Pre-Calculus
- ☐ Statistics
- ☐ Trigonometry
- ☐ _____
- ☐ _____

CTAE:

- ☐ Accounting
- ☐ Auto Repair
- ☐ Business
- ☐ Computer Science
- ☐ Cosmetology
- ☐ Culinary Arts
- ☐ Entrepreneurship
- ☐ Fashion Design
- ☐ Graphic Design
- ☐ Healthcare
- ☐ JROTC
- ☐ Law/Criminal Justice
- ☐ Marketing
- ☐ Music Production
- ☐ Nutrition
- ☐ Robotics
- ☐ Web Design
- ☐ Welding
- ☐ Wood Working
- ☐ _____
- ☐ _____

Science:

- ☐ Anatomy & Physiology
- ☐ Astronomy
- ☐ Biology
- ☐ Botany
- ☐ Chemistry
- ☐ Earth Science
- ☐ Environmental Science
- ☐ Forensic Science
- ☐ Life Science
- ☐ Oceanography
- ☐ Organic Chemistry
- ☐ Physical Science
- ☐ Physics
- ☐ Zoology
- ☐ _____
- ☐ _____

Physical Education:

- ☐ Aerobics
- ☐ Gymnastics
- ☐ Health
- ☐ Physical Education
- ☐ Swimming
- ☐ Wellness
- ☐ Weight Training
- ☐ _____
- ☐ _____

Visual Arts:

- ☐ Art
- ☐ Art History
- ☐ Digital Media
- ☐ Drawing
- ☐ Film Production/Video
- ☐ Photography
- ☐ _____
- ☐ _____

Social Studies:

- ☐ American History
- ☐ Anthropology
- ☐ Current Events
- ☐ Economics
- ☐ European History
- ☐ Geography
- ☐ International Relations
- ☐ Political Science
- ☐ Psychology
- ☐ Religious Studies
- ☐ Sociology
- ☐ US Government
- ☐ World History
- ☐ World Religions
- ☐ _____
- ☐ _____

Performing Arts:

- ☐ Choir
- ☐ Concert Band
- ☐ Dance
- ☐ Drama
- ☐ Jazz Band
- ☐ Music Theory
- ☐ Orchestra
- ☐ _____
- ☐ _____

Dual-Enrollment Courses:

- ☐ _____
- ☐ _____
- ☐ _____
- ☐ _____
- ☐ _____
- ☐ _____

Student Notes

CHAPTER 6

BUILDING YOUR COLLEGE & CAREER PLAN

Now that you know what you should be doing for your sophomore year and how colleges work, you will need to begin building your College & Career plan. In order to build an effective plan, you will need to document your current and planned activities, and periodically assess your progress towards your plan. You will need to be mindful of your activities and how you compare to your peers. Below, is a sophomore's five-step plan:

Step 1: Identify who can currently assist you throughout this process. You should have created a small list of individuals that you can contact in the student profile at the beginning of this workbook. At this time, I want you to think of any other people that you can add to the list. Consider someone at school, church, a student or youth group, a family member, etc. It is important to have a team to support you in this process. Your most relevant supporters will change as you matriculate through high school, and that's to be expected. Input their name in your supporter list in the Sophomore College Plan section of the workbook.

Step 2: Lay out a timeline of activities that you will commit to throughout your sophomore year. Examples of activities may include: researching college admissions requirements at a few colleges, looking for scholarships offered to high school sophomores, participating in a college fair at your school, attending an essay writing workshop, etc. Use the calendar and journal forms in the Sophomore College Plan section of the workbook to plan and document your activities by month.

Step 3: Begin to make yourself a highly-sought-after student. To do this, you will need to continue participating in activities that will fill up your student brag sheet. Get involved in extracurricular activities worth talking about, try to attain a leadership role in organizations, and create opportunities where you may be recognized. Take some time to think about what you have done to add to the Student Brag Sheet. Each time you have a new accomplishment or activity, be sure to add it as well.

Step 4: Begin researching colleges that you have heard of or might be interested in. It's never too early to learn about options for your future. Take the time to start looking into what colleges have to offer. During your spring break or the summer between your sophomore and junior years, take a visit to at least one college. Begin the process to understand what a college campus feels like.

Step 5: Start researching how your potential college choices can assist you in getting to your potential career goals. You have to determine if the colleges offer the programs that lead to your intended career. Some colleges may not have the major, but could potentially have a way for you to get to your goal.

(Ex: You want to be an engineer. College A doesn't have an engineering program. However, they have a partnership with College B that allows you transfer after taking **core courses**. This may be a good option for some students to take advantage of. However, you have to do the research to find out if it would be a good fit for you.

Using The College & Career Plan

The College & Career Plan is very important for a sophomore student. At this time, you have one full year of high school under your belt. The stakes aren't as high as the juniors and seniors. However, this is the perfect time to create a plan for what you will do with the remaining time you have in high school. Here is how to use the College & Career Plan section of the workbook:

As you will notice, the plan is comprised of a calendar, journal, and results page for each month. This will be your way of documenting important dates for the academic year and summer, college and career activities you have completed and are planning to pursue, as well as a way to identify what you have learned along the way.

The first thing we must do is identify your overall goals. Think about it, and be very specific.

What is your current post-secondary goal?

_____

_____

_____

What is your current career goal?

_____

_____

_____

Who are your current top 5 supporters through this process?

1. _____ Relationship: _____

How? _____

2. _____ Relationship: _____

How? _____

3. _____ Relationship: _____

How? _____

4. _____ Relationship: _____

How? _____

5. _____ Relationship: _____

How? _____

Month: _____ **Year:** _____

Monday	Tuesday	Wednesday	Thursday	Friday	Saturday	Sunday

Notes:

Monthly Journal

Date	Activity	Notes

Monthly Results

Notes/What Have You Learned?

Monthly Results

Notes/What Have You Learned?

Month:					Year:	
Monday	**Tuesday**	**Wednesday**	**Thursday**	**Friday**	**Saturday**	**Sunday**
	Notes:					

Monthly Journal

Date	Activity	Notes

Monthly Results

Notes/What Have You Learned?

Month: _____					Year: _____	
Monday	**Tuesday**	**Wednesday**	**Thursday**	**Friday**	**Saturday**	**Sunday**
	Notes:					

Monthly Journal

Date	Activity	Notes

Monthly Results

Notes/What Have You Learned?

Month: _____ Year: _____

Monday	Tuesday	Wednesday	Thursday	Friday	Saturday	Sunday

Notes:

Monthly Journal

Date	Activity	Notes

Monthly Results

Notes/What Have You Learned?

Month: _____					Year: _____	
Monday	**Tuesday**	**Wednesday**	**Thursday**	**Friday**	**Saturday**	**Sunday**
Notes:						

Monthly Journal

Date	Activity	Notes

Monthly Results

Notes/What Have You Learned?

Month: _____ **Year:** _____

Monday	Tuesday	Wednesday	Thursday	Friday	Saturday	Sunday
	Notes:					

Monthly Journal

Date	Activity	Notes

Monthly Results

Notes/What Have You Learned?

Month:				Year:		
Monday	**Tuesday**	**Wednesday**	**Thursday**	**Friday**	**Saturday**	**Sunday**
	Notes:					

Monthly Journal

Date	Activity	Notes

Monthly Results

Notes/What Have You Learned?

Month:				Year:		
Monday	**Tuesday**	**Wednesday**	**Thursday**	**Friday**	**Saturday**	**Sunday**

Notes:

Monthly Journal

Date	Activity	Notes

Monthly Results

Notes/What Have You Learned?

Month:					Year:	
Monday	**Tuesday**	**Wednesday**	**Thursday**	**Friday**	**Saturday**	**Sunday**
	Notes:					

Monthly Journal

Date	Activity	Notes

Monthly Results

Notes/What Have You Learned?

Month: _____ **Year:** _____

Monday	Tuesday	Wednesday	Thursday	Friday	Saturday	Sunday
	Notes:					

Monthly Journal

Date	Activity	Notes

Monthly Results

Notes/What Have You Learned?

Month: _____ **Year:** _____

Monday	Tuesday	Wednesday	Thursday	Friday	Saturday	Sunday

Notes:

Monthly Journal

Date	Activity	Notes

Monthly Results

Notes/What Have You Learned?

Month: _____ **Year:** _____

Monday	Tuesday	Wednesday	Thursday	Friday	Saturday	Sunday

Notes:

Monthly Journal

Date	Activity	Notes

Did you meet all of your goals this year? Explain/Elaborate.

What are your projected goals for your junior year? Explain/Elaborate.

What are your projected goals for your senior year? Explain/Elaborate.

What are your projected goals for your freshman year in college? Explain/Elaborate.

Student Notes

Glossary

Academic Scholarships - Financial awards based on academic achievement as evident in your college application.

Academic Year - The timeframe in which students will take academic courses. Generally, in high school it is August to May, with summers off. In college, the academic year runs from August to July because colleges offer summer courses.

Acceptance - The decision made by the admissions committee or department to offer the opportunity of enrollment to a student.

ACT - American College Test. A standardized college admissions test, created by ACT, Inc. it assesses students on what they have learned in class.

Advanced Placement Course - Advanced Placement or "AP" high school course that also offers college credit, if the student successfully completes the course and achieves a certain score on the post-test.

Applicant - Any student that has completed an application to an institution.

Associate Degree - An undergraduate degree awarded to students who have completed post-secondary courses, generally lasting two years. An Associate degree will require around 60 credit hours on average.

ASVAB - Armed Services Vocational Aptitude Battery. A test that will show military recruiters what vocation or job a student will be most well suited for in the military.

Athletic Scholarships - Financial awards based on athletic ability and your perspective college's departmental needs, generally given to Division I, II, and III athletes.

Bachelor's Degree - An undergraduate degree awarded to students who complete post-secondary courses lasting generally four to five years. A Bachelor's degree will require around 120 credit hours on average.

Certificate - A short undergraduate completion that is not degree-seeking. It is generally career-or- trade focused. It does not require the same amount of time or program rigor as a degree.

College Readiness - The process and activities during which students prepare for a college education. Students can take a program, read books, attend events at their high school, etc.

College Recruiter - A college employee that is tasked to travel and promote the institution to potential students and the community at large. Sometimes alumni recruiters will attend events. These individuals don't work for the college, but are highly involved with the college's alumni association. They are just as capable to answer your questions.

Core Courses - General education courses that all students have to complete before taking major courses. A student's major will determine if there are certain core courses he or she does not have to take. Examples of core courses are English, math, psychology, etc.

Cost of Attendance - The total cost of college, including tuition, room and board, books, transportation, fees, and personal expenses.

Credit Hours - The weight given in time associated with an academic course. Some courses will weigh more than others. Most college courses weigh 3 credit hours.

Demonstrated Need - Your cost of attendance minus your expected family contribution.

Developmental/Learning Support Course - A non-college level, remedial course that is designed with support activities to assist students in reaching college level course work. These courses do not count in reaching degree credit requirements and will not transfer to another school.

Dual Enrollment Program - An option that refers to students being enrolled concurrently in two distinct academic programs or educational institutions. The term is most prevalently used in reference to high school students taking college courses while they are still enrolled in a high school.

Expected Family Contribution - The amount of money you and your family could be expected to pay for one year of college costs.

Elective Courses - An optional course that a student can choose to take, unlike the required courses already designed into the program. Most programs require students to take a certain number of elective courses.

Enrolled - The process of being accepted and officially registered for a course or set of courses.

FAFSA - Free Application for Federal Student Aid, a required federal application for any student who is looking to use need-based financial aid to help pay for college, including loans, grants, and work-study, and some scholarships.

Financial Aid Package - The total amount of financial aid a student receives. Federal and non-federal aid such as grants, loans, and work-study, are combined in a "package" to help met the student's needs.

First Generation Student - A college-bound or current college student whose parents did attend college. These students may or may not need extra resources due to a lack of college experience at home.

FSA ID - Federal Student Aid ID, a unique code given to students and their parents that will give them access to their financial aid information. Students and parents will also use the FSA ID to electronically sign their FAFSA. For more information or help, you can visit www.studentaid.gov/fsaid.

Honors Course - A course that students can take in high school that has a faster pace and are more intense than the general college preparatory courses that students take.

In-State (Resident) - A student whose permanent residence is in the same state as the college or university he or she plans to attend. In-state students generally pay lower tuition rates than out-of-state students.

Institutional Scholarships - Financial awards that are offered at a particular college, or in a particular department at the college.

Major - A student's major is their designated field or program of study. Example: A student who would like to be a police officer would likely major in Criminal Justice.

Matriculation - The process of a student progressing through their educational program.

Minor - A student's minor is their secondary designated field of study. Unlike a concentration, it will be a totally separate field from their major. Example: A student who would like to be a criminal investigator can major in Criminal Justice and minor is psychology for interviewing and interpersonal skills.

NCAA - National Collegiate Athletic Association. A member-led association which regulates college level athletics.

Non-Traditional Student - A potential or current student who did not follow the traditional route of attending a college right out of high school.

Non-Traditional Program Student - A student entering into a field of study or career where 25% or less of their gender is represented in the industry. This is highly encouraged by professional associations in given fields of study. Examples of Non-Traditional program students are female students studying welding, or male students studying nursing.

Out-of-State - A student whose permanent residence is not in the same state as the college or university he or she plans to attend. Out-of-state students generally pay higher tuition rates than in-state students.

Preview Day - A common name used for a day the college has scheduled for students to visit the campus. Some colleges will have a different name for it.

Post-Secondary Education - Education after high school, also known as higher education or college education.

Private Organization Scholarships - Financial awards that can be given by many organizations including: places of worship, school districts, chambers of commerce, philanthropic organizations & foundations, business, clubs, etc.

PSAT - The Practice Scholastic Aptitude Test, Practice SAT. Students can take the PSAT for eligibility for National Merit Scholarships.

Registration - The process of enrolling into a course or set of courses.

Retention - The degree or percentage to which students will matriculate through, or remain enrolled into, a program or institution and persist to graduation.

SAT - The Scholastic Aptitude Test is a college admissions standardized test. It is created by College Board and tests student's aptitude and critical thinking skills.

Selectivity - The degree to which colleges admit or deny students based on the individual student's academic achievement. Generally, highly selective schools admit 25% of applicants, very selective schools admit 26% - 49% of applicants, selective schools admit 50% - 75% of applicants, and schools with open admissions admit applicants based on seat availability.

Semester - A unit of measurement for college courses running on a common academic year. Semesters run from August to December and January to May. Summer semesters are shorter, and the coursework is condensed to fit the timeframe.

Student Profile - A combination of data points that colleges can use to determine a student's eligibility for admission at their institution. It includes GPA, test scores, extracurricular activities, etc.

Student Ambassadors - Generally upper-class students who are interested in assisting the college with visitation days, giving campus tours, and guiding new students. This can be a paid or volunteer position.

Superscoring - The process where colleges will take a student's best section scores from multiple test dates to create one score. Superscoring only works for the same test on multiple days.

Transfer - The process of officially leaving one college to attend another college.

Undecided - A classification given to students who have not declared a major at the college.

Undergraduate - A term used to describe a student who has not completed a Bachelor's degree. This includes students progressing towards a certificate, Associate degree, and a Bachelor's degree.

Waitlist - A classification given to students who have not been accepted to the institution on the first round of application reviews.

References

Best College Reviews. (2016). *The 50 top research universities.* Retrieved from http://www. bestcollegereviews.org/top-research-universities/

Federal Student Aid. (n.d.a). *Aid for military families.* Retrieved from https://studentaid. ed.gov/sa/types/grants-scholarships/military

Grove, A. (2016). *Ivy league schools: College admissions information for some of the most elite U.S. universities.* Retrieved from http://collegeapps.about.com/od/choosingacollege/ tp/ivy-league-schools.htm

Longley, R. (2016). *Lifetime earning soar with education.* Retrieved from http://usgovinfo.about. com/od/moneymatters/a/edandearnings.htm

U.S. News and World Report. (n.d.a). *Top public schools: Regional universities.* Retrieved from http://colleges.usnews.rankingsandreviews.com/best-colleges/rankings/regional-universities/top-public

U.S. News and World Report. (n.d.b). *Undergraduate research/creative projects.* Retrieved from http://colleges.usnews.rankingsandreviews.com/best-colleges/rankings/undergrad-research-programs

College View. (n.d.). The history of historically black colleges and universities: A tradition rich in history. Retrieved from

http://www.collegeview.com/articles/article/the-history-of-historically-black-colleges-and-universities